Just Show Up

Geyers
May you always
Show Up when the
Lord calls — as you have.
Blessings
Amy Mc

Just Show Up

You Never Know Who Will Be Blessed

Andy McClure

Copyright © 2022 by Andy McClure.

Library of Congress Control Number:		2022910892
ISBN:	Hardcover	978-1-6698-2906-5
	Softcover	978-1-6698-2905-8
	eBook	978-1-6698-2904-1

All rights reserved. No part of this book may be reproduced or transmitted in any form or by any means, electronic or mechanical, including photocopying, recording, or by any information storage and retrieval system, without permission in writing from the copyright owner.

Scripture quotations marked NIV are taken from the Holy Bible, New International Version®. NIV®. Copyright © 1973, 1978, 1984 by International Bible Society. Used by permission of Zondervan. All rights reserved. [Biblica]

Any people depicted in stock imagery provided by Getty Images are models, and such images are being used for illustrative purposes only.
Certain stock imagery © Getty Images.

Print information available on the last page.

Rev. date: 06/08/2022

To order additional copies of this book, contact:
Xlibris
844-714-8691
www.Xlibris.com
Orders@Xlibris.com
809047

Contents

Dedication vii
Introduction ix

Chapter 1   August 20, 2018 1
Chapter 2   The Floodgates Opened 5
Chapter 3   Woody Allen and Image Bearers 9
Chapter 4   A Divine Relationship 17
Chapter 5   Sacrificial Responsibility 21
Chapter 6   Tyrant or Lifeless 25
Chapter 7   What Can Be Done? 33
Chapter 8   Death in the Life of a Friend or Family
            Member—Show Up 37
Chapter 9   Birth of a New Baby—Show Up 41
Chapter 10 Loss of a Job—Show Up 43
Chapter 11 Surgery—Show Up 45
Chapter 12 Your Church—Show Up 47
Chapter 13 A Friend Is Struggling—Show Up 51
Chapter 14 Helping Those at Work—Show Up 55
Chapter 15 Helping Organizations—Show Up 59
Chapter 16 Local School—Show Up 61
Chapter 17 Prison Visits—Show Up 65
Chapter 18 Your Family—Show Up 71
Chapter 19 Let's Dock This Boat 79

One Last Word	83
Resources	85
About the Author	87
Afterword	89

Dedication

To Carey, Whitney, Haley, and Casey, thank you for pushing me to be a better man, husband, dad, and grandpa. You are my Disney princesses! To Geoff, Ryan and Andrew, some superheroes don't ware capes! Hudson, you are a blessing beyond words.

Introduction

In April of 1988 I proposed marriage to my girlfriend Carey, she said yes!! I'm not sure she said yes because she wanted to be my wife or she was shocked by the question and didn't know what else to say… as we had not dated long. WOW . . . now what do I do?

Being that we met while serving in youth ministry, we were blessed to know some wise Christian counsel for premarital guidance and then started planning a wedding. Come the next January, we were now an official family. That family grew 18 months later to include our oldest daughter, Whitney. Jump three years ahead, Haley and 36 months after that, Casey. Within seven years, marriage and three daughters. I was excited, shocked and overwhelmed by how all of this unfolded.

There was some wise elders on both sides of our family that offered insight in how to do family… but there was one thing I always wanted as a dad and husband, and that was to be there for **ALL** of my girls.

My plan was to help with homework, coach, chaperone, and entertain at and plan birthday parties and school events. I would talk about life on the way to the grocery store or following sporting, drama, and musical experiences. I would teach each of the girls how to run a lawnmower, cook simple dishes, drive a car, and field a groundball. For Christmas one year, they all received a small tool kit for minor household repairs, and I explained how to use the tools. We would volunteer at church, the local rescue mission, and hospital.

I will never forget the time Whitney and Casey were traveling from Washington to Colorado for Christmas. Before take-off, they were discussing fantasy football details. An older gentleman in front asked who they were as he had never known young ladies to be so well versed in the specifics of football. He asked how they knew so much. They both quickly piped up and said, "Our dad taught us about Jesus and pass interference." He was speechless.

My desire is not to be a dad in title but one who was actively involved in their lives on physical, emotional, and spiritual planes.

Why? Because I made the conscious decision to marry the first woman I fell in love with… a woman I chose to spend the next 60 years. I have been so blessed by the family the Lord bestowed upon Carey and me. Even the men my girls married would be treated the same. Today I go to breakfast with my sons-in-law monthly just to discuss life.

Growing up, I knew too many friends and schoolmates who lived with one parent and only occasionally saw the other. The lack of guidance and mentorship was woeful.

I too lived with just one parent through most of my formative years as my father traveled six days a week, and then my parents were separated when I was between eleven and twenty. They finally divorced while I was in college. I never want that type of life for anyone.

In this book, I share a life-changing experience our family has lived through. We can all learn to be present in the critical moments of life for our family, friends, and neighbors.

I learned to show up.

Chapter 1

August 20, 2018

Have you ever been roused from bed? Barking dog, smoke detector needing a new battery, thunder and lightning, maybe a phone call?

Early Monday morning, my wife Carey, woke me from a deep sleep. "Whitney quit breathing."

"What-what-what are you talking about?"

I can sleep through most anything. But that morning, Carey quickly grabbed my attention.

Our oldest daughter recently had her secondary (lingual) tonsils removed and had been home recovering from the surgery. Her husband, Geoff, had called in a panic with the news of the unthinkable.

He seemed to awaken and noticed she had stopped breathing. He pulled her to the floor and administered CPR and dialed 911, and when they arrived, he called us. It was roughly 4:30 a.m. Hurriedly out the door, we headed to the hospital. I was still wondering, *What-What did I hear?*

Upon arriving at the ER, we were met by the hospital chaplain and ushered to the waiting room. The time was 5:15 a.m.

After waiting a few hours, we were shepherded into the ICU, where we saw Whitney hooked to more monitors and machines than one could comprehend. There was little to no response other than the noises of the hopeful lifesaving instruments.

The room was abuzz of MDs, nurses, techs, and specialists. Despite their valiant efforts, her body was shutting down. One last thought: dialysis. Before the techs could wire up their instruments, she suffered cardiac arrest. The time was 12:05 p.m. Whitney Lee breathed her last.

What-what did I just witness? While in pain a few days earlier, she was mentally sharp. She was joking and, for the most part, her normal self following the tonsillectomy. What happened in four days? Was this real?

After calling out-of-state family and friends and receiving hugs and love from those who arrived at the hospital, it was time to head home, with only the memories of Whitney Lee.

This book is inspired by this sad, sad day. The focus is not on medical procedures, medications, or trying to figure out what went wrong. But it does have to do with the *heart*.

It's about Whitney's heart and the hundreds of others who shared theirs through the week leading to her funeral and how we can all create an amazing heart statement when we *just show up*.

After many weeks of research, studies, and tests, the Centers for Disease Control in Washington DC and the Colorado Department of Health concluded that the cause of Whitney's passing was acute pneumonia due to *E. coli* infection. It was something she carried in her body for a long time. For some reason, in late August 2018, it wiped out her immune system and internal organs.

Chapter 2

The Floodgates Opened

Later That Day

Carey and I traveled the fifteen minutes from the hospital to home in near silence. As we approached our house, Carey started to weep. *Why?*

So many questions and so many answers to be sought. What do we do? What took her? What is next?

Those questions would have to wait until bedtime prayer and conversation because of what had just happened and what was about to unfold.

At the Hospital and Home

Let's back up a few hours. Within fifteen minutes of Whitney's passing, the hospital started to fill up with family and friends. Longtime neighbors, colleagues, and co-workers just showed up. Others called, and we shared the dreadful news. Many dropped what they were doing and showed up. School administrators, ministry friends, neighbors, co-workers—it was over the top! They kept coming for one reason, and that was to say "I'm sorry" and "I love you."

When we went home, others began to arrive. Food started showing up. Then there were phone calls: the president of the university where Whitney earned her bachelor's degree, the surgeon who removed her tonsils four days earlier, college friends of both Carey and me, and co-workers of our youngest daughter, who had only started as a new first-year teacher the day before.

This continued for several days. The food—*oh my*! The number of roasted chickens became uncountable. We had a flock in our refrigerator!

People kept showing up. The outpour was immense and striking.

On Wednesday, Carey, Geoff, and I then had to do the unimaginable: plan a funeral for a twenty-eight-year old daughter and wife. This gave us a surreal calm as we were able to just be quiet for a couple of hours during the process.

Then people from out of state—Arizona, Wyoming, California, Michigan, and Washington—started showing up. There was more food, more hugs, and more tears.

Oh my, we were still in store for one more outpouring of kindness and passion.

On Saturday, August 25, eight-hundred-plus people made their way to Peak to Peak High School in Lafayette, Colorado, where Whitney graduated in 2008, to say their official goodbye. The speakers that day were her husband, sisters, a school counselor, and teacher. Oh yeah, the chubby, bald guy. No one was going to deny her dad from leading the ceremony and preaching the gospel over his daughter's funeral service.

A dear friend led the congregation in song. The service ran a little over an hour, but the reception lasted another three-plus hours.

People Just Kept Showing Up

Friends we had not seen in years, ballgame officials/coaches, family, and friends from around the country. There were friends of her grandparents, a college basketball team, co-workers, athletes from years past, high school and college friends—and the Holy Spirit! They all just showed up.

There were folks who helped set up the sound system, video, the gym chairs, and reception area. There were people I had never met who arrived to help, many at the request of one dear lady. The food was abundant and awe-inspiring. Friends went out and purchased all that was needed. We never saw a bill. Someone set up a "memorial walk" of Whitney's twenty-eight years of strolling this earth.

What's the point in sharing this? There are lots of sad stories about young people passing away way before they should.

The point is people *just showed up*!

Chapter 3

Woody Allen and Image Bearers

This thought of showing up has lingered in my soul for years. Showing up is so important. It is important in ministry, family, work, and sports.

Playwright and screenwriter Woody Allen once said, *"Eighty percent of success is just showing up."*

Allen clarified that comment by saying, "My observation was that once a person actually completed a play or a novel, he was well on his way to getting it produced or published as opposed to a vast majority of people who tell me their ambition is to write, but who never strike out on the very first level and indeed write the play or book."[1]

We can plan, prep, and practice; but then comes a time to perform!

I have counseled many who never get off the bench and reach out to those in need. They plan on it, they think about it, but nothing

---

[1] Showing Up is 80 percent of Life https://quoteinvestigator.com/2013/06/10/showing-up/

comes of those plans. One woman explained to me why she never sent sympathy cards to a family member after the passing of her husband. "Well, I should still get credit as I bought the cards. I thought about sending them."

While that is a great intent, we need to do something with that thought and show up.

For the next few chapters, we are going to examine this issue. The intent is to become better neighbors and family members by merely showing up, something that just doesn't happen enough.

There are many great ideas floating on social media, Internet, or even in schools. Let's give some biblical context to this. Let's look at this issue of showing up.

---

*"In your relationships with one another, have the same mindset as Christ Jesus: Who, being in very nature God, did not consider equality with God something to be used to his own advantage; rather, he made himself nothing by taking the very nature of a **servant**, being made in human likeness. And being found in appearance as a man, he **humbled himself** by becoming obedient to death—even death on a cross!"* (Phil. 2:5–8).

The Apostle Paul was writing this letter to the church at Philippi, with the main theme being how to work and live with one another. Paul was calling on the church to keep Christ's body (the church) pure and holy. This is accomplished by being like-minded with Christ.

In earlier verses of this letter, Paul gives clear direction to this decree: *"Do nothing out of selfish ambition or vain conceit. Rather, in humility*

value others above yourselves, *not looking to your own interests but each of you to the interests of the other"* (Phil. 2:3–4).

Paul is summoning the church to look out for one another. We are not to concern ourselves with just the issues of our lives.

Sure, you need to work, rest, and eat—but what about those around you: your family, co-workers, neighbors?

The church, its people, are called to be servants to others.

The reason the church is to be servants is we are image bearers of God!

"So God created mankind in his own image, in the image of God he created them; male and female he created them" (Gen. 1:27).

We are to be servants, take care of others, and value others above ourselves. That is what the Lord calls us to be.

The church is called to be servants for God. Paul was a true servant of God.

His last letter written to his mentee, Timothy, while in prison encouraged Timothy to carry on the work of the ministry with all faith and diligence. He wrote, *"Preach the word; be prepared in season and out of season; correct, rebuke and encourage—with great patience and careful instruction. For the time will come when people will not put up with sound doctrine. Instead, to suit their own desires, they will gather around them a great number of teachers to say what their itching ears want to hear. They will turn their ears away from the truth and turn aside to myths. But you, keep your head in all situations, endure hardship, do the work of an evangelist, discharge all the duties of your ministry. For I am already being poured out like a drink offering, and the time for my departure is near. I have fought the good fight, I have finished the race, I have kept the faith. Now there is in store for me the crown of righteousness, which the Lord, the righteous Judge, will award to me on that day—and not only to me, but also to all who have longed for his appearing"* (2 Tim. 4:2–8).

Who goes to their grave with this proclamation? I should have spent more time at work! Can you imagine coming to the end and saying, "Wow, if I had only served my family better, been a more courteous neighbor, reached out to my extended family more often, shared the gospel to those who didn't know. I wish I would have shown up when it mattered!"

God, the creator of the heavens and earth, tells *his* kingdom that they are servants because we were created in his image. God placed into our lives everything we need to survive—air, water, food, and love—to sustain life and provide for those in need. Yet we have trouble coming alongside those in need and at times distressed. *Why?*

This smacks against the image our American or Western cultured society's beliefs and expectations. There is such an "I earned this, this is mine, and they don't deserve my time" attitude that many both outside and inside the church only vaguely resemble the directive of Paul, which is to humbly value others above yourselves.

We are selfish, and that is *sin*!

We value who we are more than we value others. This is an issue the Apostle Paul spoke about two thousand years ago. It is an issue we still face today. Just look at the war, divorce, theft, and infidelity that surround us. People are acting with a "me first, my way" attitude.

I know too many people who never write a check, volunteer at a charity or school, or assist their neighbor with a task around the house. Many of them even call themselves Christians.

It is surprising that there is a move developing in public and private colleges and universities on this issue. Several schools don't just offer classes but also provide full academic degrees in servant leadership. These schools include Gonzaga, Liberty, Cornell, and Boise State.[2]

There are others, but there is such a need to develop servants that both secular and Christian universities are working to rekindle the idea that mankind was created to serve one another.

It's Not Just about Me!

One of my favorite authors/speakers is Pastor Max Lucado. Max addresses this issue in his book *It's Not about Me*. The sad truth is too many in the church believe it is about them.

---

[2] Servant Leadership, Cornell College https://online.cornell.edu/leadership?creative =448080217352&keyword=%2Bleadership%20%2Bclass&matchtype=b& network=s&device=c&utm_campaign=ldrshp_US+-+BMM+-+Leadership+ General&utm_source=google&utm_medium=cpc&utm_term=%2Bleadership %20%2Bclass&utm_content=g_448080217352_b&creative=448080217352& keyword=%2Bleadership%20%2Bclass&matchtype=b&nehttps%3A%2F%2 Fonline.cornell.edu%2Fleadership%3Fcreative%3D448080217352%26keyword %3D%252Bleadership%2520%252Bclass%26matchtype%3Db%26network %3Ds%26device%3Dc&target=&position=&gclid=Cj0KCQjw7MGJBhD-ARIsAMZ0eev8Pef5wL0bEMeyOhIhGMB2pe4UReCjD9pXBX1DbRD-NzyPP3vkOSMaAjmaEALw_wcB

Max writes, "We've been demanding our way since day one. 'I want a spouse that makes me happy and co-workers that always ask my opinion.' 'I want weather that suits me and traffic that helps me and government that serves me.'"[3]

Self-promotion. Self-preservation. Self-centeredness.

My father-in-law, Del, was one to serve his neighborhood. If there was an issue with a car, lawnmower, garage door—you name it—he was the one people sought. He knew what he was doing, and he loved serving those who needed the help. He understood the gifts and talents he was blessed with, and he used them to serve others. He was a VP at a noted aerospace company. This work was not below him. He knew he was called to serve. Have socket wrench and pliers will travel!

Robert Greenleaf created the Center for Servant Leadership in Atlanta to address this issue. *He suggests that when someone is serving another, the test of service is to determine if there's growth in the one being served.* [4]

It is one thing to give or dump on someone what you "think they need," but is it helpful? Did they grow or find healing from that information or experience? Are they blessed, or are they comforted? Was it servanthood well placed?

Robert Lupton, in his book *Toxic Charity*, shares that the American church many times hurts those they are serving around the world.

---

[3] It's Not About Me, Max Lucado, 2004, Thomas Nelson Incorporated, ISBN-10 159145042x

[4] https://www.greenleaf.org/

It seems too many share the mentality of "we know what is best for you," and we don't consider their actual needs.[5]

Lupton writes, "Because, as compassionate people, we have been evaluating our charity by the rewards we receive through service, rather than the benefits received by the served. We have failed to adequately calculate the effects of our service on the lives of those reduced to objects of our pity and patronage."

My youngest daughter, Casey, and I have spent some time working in international missions. One time, while working in South America with Habitat for Humanity, we only had hand tools to trench and build a foundation for a new house. It was hard work to dig with simple shovels.

A member of our crew was obsessed in finding a backhoe to do the digging. Great idea—by American standards. But it would have left all the digging to one person, not the group who traveled over five thousand miles to help this family. A backhoe would have eliminated much of the collegial work planned over a couple of days. It would have left many standing and watching. It also would mean leveling trees and shrubs to maneuver the backhoe into a spot.

Fellowship and community won out! This project helped our US group south of the equator to build relationships with the family and friends of this young couple and their daughter. It was not about speed or American ingenuity.

---

[5] Toxic Charity- How the Church Hurts Those They Help and How to Reverse It, Robert D. Lupton, HarperOne, Print ISBN: 9780062076212, 0062076213, 2011

When we do give, is it something the recipient really needs? Does it help build community? Or is it something that just makes us feel good?

Chapter 4

A Divine Relationship

In Ephesians 5:22–33, Paul compares the union of husband and wife to that of the relationship between Christ and the church. This passage has met with tremendous push back as some feel it is "sexist" or "oppressive." Not true. (This is a discussion for another time.) Men and women have different roles but the same goal, which is to serve one another.

Paul calls men to "*love their wives as Christ LOVED the church, and gave himself up for her to make her holy*" (Eph. 5:25–26a).

The word *love* here is ἀγαπᾶτε or *agape* in English. This is different than Eros or Philia love.

Eros is the Greek word that describes romantic or sexual love. The term also portrays the idea of passion and intensity of feeling. But it can also become a selfish love: get what you can, enjoy it, and then move on. This is where we get the word *erotic*. All can be good in the right context.

Eros love can also be used in our "lust" for things.

This type of love can be for cheesecake! "Oh, I love cheesecake. It makes me happy!" Too much, and you push it away. It served *my* purpose, and now, I am done with it. Very one sided. Man can't serve a cheesecake, but a cheesecake can serve man.

In its proper place, Eros is good, but our sinful world often moves this to something dirty and immoral.

Philia is a brotherly love or caring for a friend. It is the most general form of love in the Bible, encompassing love for fellow humans: care, respect, and compassion for people in need. The most common form of philia is friendship. The city Philadelphia is known as the City of Brotherly Love. It is a love for the co-worker or neighbor. You most likely won't go too far out of your way to serve them, but when there is a crisis, you will reach out and help. Your personal sacrifice may have limits.

Agape is how Christ served and loved the church: the self-sacrificing love of God for humanity. This is the love a man should have for his wife, as well as the rest of his family and community, giving all of you for the other—sacrifice. This is the love that Paul was referring to in the Ephesians passage about husbands and wives.

C. S. Lewis writes in *The Four Loves,* that agape "is the love that exists regardless of changing circumstances."[6] It is a commitment to someone that will never be broken, no matter what circumstances may arise.

---

[6] https://en.wikipedia.org/wiki/The_Four_Loves

In Paul's writing, he is referring to the Gen 2:22–24 passage: *"This is now bone of my bones and flesh of my flesh; she shall be called 'woman,' for she was taken out of man. That is why a man leaves his father and mother and is united to his wife, and they become one flesh."* They are one!

The church, the people, is the bride to Christ's bridegroom. The relationship is to be as intimate as a married couple! The one-flesh union between husband and wife means they are now one body so that the care a husband has for his wife he has for himself, and the care a wife has for her husband is for herself.

They are one. What he does to her he does to himself. Christ loves His church until death! He humbled himself by becoming obedient to death—even death on a cross!

Just as the husband is one flesh with his wife, so is the church one body with Christ. When the husband cherishes and cares for his wife, he cherishes and cares for himself; and when Christ cherishes and cares for the church, He cherishes and cares for Himself.

So if Christ humbled Himself for His church, we should do the same: humble ourselves for the sake of the church, its people!

We are called to *show up* and serve those who have been entrusted to us the same way Christ showed up and sacrificed Himself for the salvation of the world.

Chapter 5

Sacrificial Responsibility

As *image bearers*, we are called to show up and serve others because that is what God did at creation. He gave mankind all they needed to prosper. Even in the opening chapter of the gospel of John, at creation, God gave us Jesus to be the sacrifice for our sin in the garden and the multitude of sins in our personal lives.

If we truly act as image bearers/servants, then the world would be a utopia.

Wars would cease, political rhetoric would be unifying, hunger would be eliminated, and divorce would be a thought of the past.

But that is not the case.

We discover this through chapter 3 of Genesis. Adam and Eve disobeyed God, and now, all mankind is paying the price. The Lord God said to the woman, *"What is this you have done?' The woman said, 'The serpent deceived me, and I ate'"* (Gen. 3:13).

Eve is not the only one to blame here. Adam proclaimed, *"The woman you put here with me—she gave me some fruit from the tree, and I ate it"* (Gen. 3:12). Adam pointed his finger at Eve and made the claim she was the one at fault. Adam is also to blame here. The God of Creation instructed Adam about the dangers of the "tree" (Gen. 2:15–17). Adam was given the command not to eat before Eve was even birthed. He knew the rules, yet he didn't do anything to protect her from the serpent. In the big picture, both are to blame. All are to blame.

We are not the humble servants God calls us to be because of the selfish acts within our lives, just like Adam and Eve.

This is original sin, and it stems from Adam and Eve's rebellion in Eden—the sin of disobedience in consuming the forbidden fruit from the tree of the knowledge of good and evil.

To sin is to do something that is opposed by God or not do something that God calls us to do, which is to *show up*.

From the beginning, man has not lived the life that God calls him to. Showing up can be uncomfortable, so most people do everything to avoid it.

Author and lecturer Doug Wilson speaks to that by calling the church to take its proper role of servant. He calls this the glad assumption of sacrificial responsibility.[7]

---

[7] Masculinity Is the Glad Assumption of Responsibility, https://vimeo.com/30751344

While Doug uses this statement to define Christian masculinity, I believe the case can be made for both genders.

When we own that all of mankind was created as image bearers of God/servants, then we are also stating that we will gladly assume sacrificial responsibility for that which is around us or those we have been entrusted.

The problem is we make excuses: "I'm busy," "I have too many commitments," "I have to work," "At least I thought about it," "My favorite TV show is on," "I need a break," "My kids have ball practice," "Sunday is my only day off," "I worked hard for my money. I should decide how to use it," "People aren't thankful when I do help." What will I get back?" "I don't like to be rejected," or "I'm not sure what to say or do."

Wow, this is just scratching the surface of excuses. Sadly, some of these I have used and others are ones I have heard by those in the church and outside. We are called to show up—no excuses.

Chapter 6

Tyrant or Lifeless

For several years, while serving as a youth pastor, I had students who participated in church youth group or confirmation classes. Unfortunately, some parents arrived late for pickup. Many times, they arrived an hour or so after our event was over.

Sure, they *showed up*, but it was late. "My TV show was on" or "I needed a break"—they thought of themselves over others and forced the staff to wait for their arrival. They hailed themselves over several people because they knew they could get away with it.

This is called bullying or autocracy. These are those who care for themselves at the expense of others. They overuse their power or social status and have a "keeper of the car keys/money/rules" mentality.

There were times I needed to get home on time, so I drove the students of the tardy parents home. There were parents who were very apologetic and appreciative. Others were angry that I "showed them up" in front of their middle schooler. One father felt that I overstepped my role by bringing his son home despite being an hour late. Not sure why I was the bad guy. Oh yes, he has a bully's heart!

Was he Genghis Khan, Kim Jong-un, or Ivan the Terrible? No, not to that level, but we are called to be the image bearers of God, not ones to speak down to those deemed below us to or abdicate our sacrificial responsibility called for in the scripture. This has become too common in workplaces, homes, sports teams, neighborhood clubs, and the like.

I work a great deal in sports, mainly with the NCAA, high school, and club sports groups. I know hundreds of coaches across the United States, most of whom are great people on and off the court. They go out of their way to coach, teach, and mentor their athletes and staff. I have been included in several "team building" events of programs: dinners, gift exchanges, movie nights, and the like. I am thankful to get to know coaches and their players more intimately. But a few go rouge and destroy the mindset and spirit of their players. Why? They need to get what they want, and the athlete they are responsible for is the target of their overuse of power.

When a coach or leader like this do show up, the agenda is theirs; and if they don't receive the results, they are seeking, someone will pay. I see this at all levels: college, high school, and youth sports. This does not happen often, but when it does, it is ugly.

I have been called by school athletic directors and conference administrators seeking my opinion as they are about to "pull the plug" on a rogue coach.

Many who act this way carry the mentality of "I'm here helping you! You need to respect me, do what I say, and act as I expect. It is a privilege for you to have me as your coach." It becomes all about themselves.

Interesting. I have never had a call about a coach who is upstanding in their ways with the game, players, and those surrounding an event. Never. Those witnessing this behavior understand the sacrifice that the coach is making for their team, school, and fans! It is what is expected. It should be the norm. There is no need to reel them in!

I have sent emails and letters and left messages for school administrators, commissioners, and other coaches about the coaches who truly *show up* and serve their team, their families, and the school they represent! Some have raced to the rescue of an injured athlete not on their team and have been the first to congratulate the winner in a single game or championship tournament. They are a true blessing to watch in action!

I have seen bosses who rule with an iron fist and demand "the world" from those under their care. Sadly, they then expect grace and mercy when their shortcomings find the light of day. When this becomes the norm, you will witness frequent staff turnovers, lots of gripping among the staff, and people routinely calling out sick.

The flipside of this is something just as injurious. This is the issue of passivity or apathy.

Passivity is the personality that says, "All which is bad or those in need are *not my problem*. They got themselves into this mess. Let them figure how to get out."

If someone is sick, hungry, and naked, we are called to show up and help remedy the situation.

This is Matthew 25:31–46. Picking up Jesus's words at verse 37, *"then the righteous will answer him, 'Lord, when did we see you hungry and feed you, or thirsty and give you something to drink? When did we see you a stranger and invite you in, or needing clothes and clothe you? When did we see you sick or in prison and go to visit you?' The King will reply, 'Truly I tell you, whatever you did for one of the least of these brothers and sisters of mine, you did for me.'"*

This is the description of the sheep. Then, there are the goats:

> *Then he will say to those on his left, "Depart from me, you who are cursed, into the eternal fire prepared for the devil and his angels. For I was hungry and you gave me nothing to eat, I was thirsty and you gave me nothing to drink, I was a stranger and you did not invite me in, I needed clothes and you did not clothe me, I was sick and in prison and you did not look after me." They also will answer, "Lord, when did we see you hungry or thirsty or a stranger or needing clothes or sick or in prison, and did not help you?" He will reply, "Truly I tell you, whatever you did not do for one of the least of these, you did not do for me." Then they will go away to eternal punishment, but the righteous to eternal life.*

Some will say that the way you treat the sick, elderly, imprisoned, animals, and youth is a strong indication of your salvation. We are all sinners in God's eyes. Some sins are just not as visible as others.

I'm not questioning someone's salvation, but in the words of Jesus, "When you do for the least, you are doing it for Me!"

God is the ultimate judge; but when we don't show up, we are not acting as image bearers, servants, or one with Christ.

When someone throws around Bible verses or theological ideals, it is just maybe a way to seek plaudits for their assumed righteousness. Too often, it is a smokescreen. People don't care about what you believe or know. They care about how you act and serve.

Sounding pious and righteous is something Jesus fought against.

In Matthew 23:2-7, we find the words of Jesus as he spoke to the crowd and His disciples:

> *The Pharisees and the teachers of the Law are experts in the Law of Moses. So obey everything they teach you, but don't do as they do. After all, they say one thing and do something else. They pile heavy burdens on people's shoulders and won't lift a finger to help. Everything they do is just to show off in front of others. They even make a big show of wearing Scripture verses on their foreheads and arms, and they wear big tassels for everyone to see. They love the best seats at banquets and the front seats in the meeting places. And when they are in the market, they like to have people greet them as their teachers.*

This is passive aggressive. They know what needs to be done and demand it to be done, but they are never the ones to reach out and offer a helping hand.

When we are passive in child rearing, children will make up their rules and standards.

I have sat with many families where this is the case, and the parents are thunderstruck by the behavior of their children: drinking, drugging, sleeping around, stealing, fighting, and even committing murder.

When kids are left on their own, they go out and create something greater than themselves that provides care and relationship. They are looking for love and acceptance. No, not all children will create mayhem or break laws, but they will seek love and validation elsewhere.

When a community does not have the means to employ, instruct, or guide young men and women, they will turn to something else; and frequently, it is not good.

Passive teaching is non-teaching. It leads to other issues of concern.

Too often, young ladies are willing to give away sex as they are seeking love, and young men are willing to give a little love to receive that sex. For nearly forty years, I have watched this play out. Yes, I have called dads to discuss the behaviors of their sons and daughters. Many are oblivious or downplay it as "kids will be kids." Parents are not showing up in these moments, leading to short-lived relationships with dire consequences, broken dreams, lost identities, and sometimes unexpected pregnancies.

Parents need to show up and discuss proper male/female behavior. Show up. Don't walk away when it is hard or emotional. This is when you are needed the most. That ball of string in the garage that needs to be rewound can wait!

Passivity leads to destruction in our communities.

When I was young, and now as an adult, I know too many families where the dad is not present because of too much work, divorce, or other outside interests. I'm not picking on dads as women can also become preoccupied. *But* absentee dads are far more abundant than wayward moms. I know many fathers who show up at birthdays and ball games, but not when there was homework to be done, discipline is to be administered, chores to be accomplished, or when life lessons should be taught. They are not to be found. Since no standard is being set, the kids make up the rules as they go along. Many times, absentee dads create the same results, and most of the time, they are not good. I am not trying to beat up dads, but the reality is, *many* teachable moments fall to the margins.

I grew up in a "hands off" world. Unlike my sisters, I had a huge blessing from a pastor and his wife who mentored me from late high school to post college. Will and Aletha *showed up*!

Will and I spoke regularly during those years. We talked about our lives, church business, and the upcoming Sunday worship. Will was speaking into my heart about the role of ministry that is still very prominent in my life today. We don't chat as often today, but in his late eighties, he keeps *showing up*.

When Carey and I married, I made the commitment to actively participate in my children's lives. I took on the glad assumption of sacrificial responsibility.

This meant bedtime took thirty to forty-five minutes to sing songs, tell stories, and share our lives. This meant when running errands,

I would take one or all three girls with me. The life lessons shared and learned are too numerous to count. This meant that I would coach my daughters' teams, chaperone their events, serve as team dad, drive for speech/debate events, and help host team happenings and birthday parties. Recently, this has become the norm with our grandson. When we have the blessing of watching him overnight, at bedtime, we sing songs, play silly games, and laugh and giggle. I know he should be in bed, but I also know that I need to show up in his life and be present. Laugh, cry, sing, and enjoy each other.

Today, I can honestly say there is *nothing* that I can't discuss with my wife and daughters. They can call or show up at the house. They know if they have a question or concern, Mom and Dad are there to fill in the answer or provide a shoulder to weep upon.

The key to this, start early. Middle school is too late. High school is way too late. Even if it is late in the game, you can still show up and provide love (agape) and care to those the Lord has placed in your life.

I have met too many parents who want to know the secret when they are in the eleventh hour of raising their children toward adulthood. It is the same as most things in life: show up early. You don't introduce sports into the life of your child when they are in high school if you expect them to be a collegiate or pro athlete. You start with the basics in early or elementary school. This is the same with *all aspects of life*.

If your children are grown, you can still love and nurture them in appropriate ways, keeping in mind that they are adults. You also have a second chance with your grandchildren.

Chapter 7

What Can Be Done?

It's easier to turn away and pretend we don't see the suffering of those around us: the lonely child sitting by themselves at lunch, the homeless man living on the street, or a friend losing a loved one. I know it is uncomfortable to enter into someone else's suffering, but that is our calling.

Not showing up can be as hurtful as showing up and saying something stupid.

Yes, showing up can be overwhelming too. Some days, it feels like there is enough on our plates, and bearing the weight of someone else's burden just seems like too much. It's scary to ask "How are you?" and really wait to hear the answer.

I love this story of a young boy and an older gentleman who lived as neighbors:

> One afternoon, a father watched as his young son was making his way home from the neighbor's house.

The elderly gentleman had just lost his wife to a long battle with cancer. The dad asked, "What were you doing over there?"

The boy answered, "Not much."

The dad became a little concerned and asked again, "What were you doing at the neighbor's?"

"Not much" was again the answer.

"Okay," the dad said, "do you watch TV or play games?"

"No," said the young man, "most of the time, I sit in his lap, and we just cry."

That little boy showed up!

When pain and suffering enter into our lives, many times, words fail us. The odds are we won't make it better by anything we can say. But we can be there. We can just *show up*.

For nearly two years, I was blessed to travel the United States on behalf of a Colorado organization called Rachel's Challenge. Rachel Joy Scott was the first person shot and killed at Columbine High School on April 20, 1999. The Columbine shooting was, at the time, the worst school shooting in US history and prompted a national debate on gun control and school safety, as well as a major investigation to determine what motivated the gunmen.

One month after the shooting, Darrell Scott, Rachel's father, was invited to speak to Congress about the issues of violence in America. Most thought he would speak on gun control. Nope.

He spoke about how his daughter was a strong advocate of kindness and compassion for the marginalized students of her school.

Darrell's challenge was America needs a change of heart!

This is the hallmark of Rachel's Challenge: "Compassion is the greatest form of love humans have to offer." Darrell, his wife Sandy, their children, and dozens of other speakers have traveled the world with this message.

To date, they have spoken to tens of millions of junior and senior high school students, staff, administrators and community leaders here in the United States and globally.

Several years ago, Darrell shared with me and several other speakers, "To me, it's cultivating an atmosphere, a climate and a culture where everyone's accepted, because when people feel accepted, they're not going to do something like Eric and Dylan did."

Their efforts have saved the lives of numerous students who were about to commit suicide. The message of Rachel's Challenge has struck down gang violence and fights. It has also kept several individuals from committing heinous acts like what happened at Columbine High School.

It was an honor to speak to about one hundred thousand people from Southern California to Maine, sharing words of hope, kindness, and compassion.

Rachel's Challenge shows up. What are you doing?

Today, the world suffers from natural disasters, regional wars, famine, and neglect. There are groups like the Salvation Army, the International Red Cross, Habitat for Humanity, All Hands, Samaritan's Purse, and World Vision that provide emergency assistance including mass and mobile feeding, temporary shelter, counseling, missing-person services, medical assistance, and distribution of donated goods, including food, clothing, and household items.

They also provide referrals to government and private agencies for special services. These groups are also experts in providing clean-up and rebuilding assistance, especially to the elderly, disabled, widowed, and those least able to help themselves.

They are great. They show up, but what are *you* doing?

Right now, you have a chance to make a difference in your school, neighborhood, and family by showing up and providing love, kindness, and compassion to someone in need. Here are some things to consider.

Chapter 8

Death in the Life of a Friend or Family Member—Show Up

After Whitney's death, many people shared with me that they let me have my space or didn't want to get in my face, or they didn't know what to say or do when she passed away.

Stepping into a vulnerable moment is risky. We don't offer classes on how to deal with life when someone dies until after they have passed away. Here is the simplest thing you can do:

Show up, give them a hug, tell them you're sorry, and weep with them.

That's it!

You don't have to have a planned speech or some theological explanation as to why Grandma or Dad or a child died.

Over time, I have collected thoughts and phrases to share with people regarding loss and grief.

The Best Things to Say to Someone in Grief

1. I am so sorry for your loss.
2. I wish I had the right words. Just know I care.
3. I don't know how you feel, but I am here to help in any way I can.
4. You and your loved one will be in my thoughts and prayers.
5. My favorite memory of your loved one is . . .
6. I am always just a phone call away.
7. Give a hug instead of saying something.
8. We all need help at times like this. I am here for you.
9. I am usually up early or late if you need anything.
10. Say nothing. Just be with the person.

The Worst Things to Say to Someone in Grief

1. At least she lived a long life. Many people die young.
2. He/she is in a better place.
3. Did she bring this on herself?
4. There is a reason for everything.
5. Aren't you over him yet? He has been dead for a while.
6. You can still have another child.
7. She was such a good person God wanted her to be with Him.
8. I know how you feel (unless you have suffered a similar loss).
9. She did what she came here to do, and it was her time to go.
10. Be strong.

Many great friends and family members just gave us a shoulder to cry upon. Then others didn't know what to do say or do, so they used a line from the second list. Little did they know they made things worse.

I know many well-meaning Christians who just didn't know what to say, so they offer a cliché that sounds good.

The worst three statements I have heard many times since Whitney's passing were "God needed her more than you did," "God needed another angel," and "When will you be over this?" Sounds good? Nope. Painful!

I'm going to hit this again:

Show up, hug, and weep with your friend or family member.

No words needed.

You can also help with funeral plans where needed and then show up at the service and help with the setup and tear down. Be there for those grieving the loss.

Show up and do some housework: do the dishes or laundry, as well as clean the stove and counters. Not huge issues but meaningful for the one with the loss.

The week between Whitney's passing and funeral, we witnessed at least a dozen kitchen and bathroom scrubbings. Yes, you could eat off our floors! Our bathrooms were scrubbed, laundry washed, folded, and put away. People just showed up and did!

One last time: if you don't know what to say, say nothing. Give a hug and weep with the one grieving.

Chapter 9

Birth of a New Baby—Show Up

This is tricky. Is the baby okay? Is the mom okay? How long will they be in the hospital? All great questions, but there are many ways you can show up and serve someone you love and not have to make the trip to the hospital.

Make dinner for the family or check on dietary issues. This can be huge. It is not that someone can't afford the meal. It is the gesture. New moms and dads can be inundated with all the issues of dealing with a new baby. Making dinner for the family can become an afterthought.

If the family has other children, offer to run them around to/from school, sports/dance activities, or even to and from the hospital to visit their new sibling.

Offer and show up to scrub the kitchen and bathrooms. A couple of friends did this for us when our girls were born. They didn't ask. They just showed up and went to work. What a blessing!

If it is the proper season, just show up and mow the lawn, blow out the gutters, and wash down the driveway and sidewalk. In the spring and summer, lawn issues can get out of hand in a week or so. In the winter, shovel the snow! It's a terrible job, but you can show up and do it. Again, what a godsend.

Chapter 10

Loss of a Job—Show Up

Many people are not so prone to share this information. But if you are a true friend, you know when this happens.

Invite them over for a meal and fellowship time. You can also take them to breakfast or lunch and introduce them to someone in their line of work who may have an opportunity or some leads on new work.

They may need to vent, and you can be that sympathetic, empathetic ear.

Don't inundate them with job offers or opportunities. They may not be ready for stacks of information yet. Don't give them advice as to why this might have happened unless they ask. Give them a little space to figure out what they want to do. Once they do, take their kids when they have interviews, need to update résumés, or make phone calls to prospective bosses.

Seek out job recruiters or head hunters in their line of work. Present the information at the proper time.

You may also file through your list of friends who work in similar fields who may be able to present a résumé to their employer on your friend's behalf.

Can you open a door to the next job opportunity? If the loss is the result of bad behavior or mismanagement, maybe you can offer counsel or send them to a job coach. Many churches are now offering this service. It is not always about what we know. Many times, it is who we know that may open the next door.

My wife, Carey, has opened this door several times. There are groups and agencies that offer these services, many times for free, and she has guided them to the proper folks who can guide those seeking a job.

In our nonprofit, we have only hired those we or others on our team have had a longtime relationship. Many managers will hire someone on a personal recommendation over someone else who may have more experience.

One last thought on this one: if you are a person of financial means, you could offer a short-term loan to help your friend get to the next job.

Chapter 11

Surgery—Show Up

The odds are you can't "go back" with a friend or extended family member while they are facing surgery. This is usually limited to immediate family.

Today most surgeries are outpatient, so the stay in the hospital is only a few hours.

But you can, as mentioned before, make a meal.

You can be the "bus driver" to and from the hospital or clinic.

If the patient is elderly, they may not have children available to check up on them during the day. And if they have children, they may work and not be available. You can sit with them, read to them, and watch TV with them. Just be present.

You can also pick up meds at the hospital or pharmacy. This could be an ongoing issue if the patient is not capable of driving or walking.

Pick up their mail, run the vacuum, wipe down the kitchen counters, or roll out the weekly trash pickup.

You can show up by running errands, dry cleaning, pet issues, DMV Tags (double bonus here), grocery shopping.

Chapter 12

Your Church—Show Up

Yes, we should all be actively involved in a local church. We need to continually hear the word of God and offer our worship and praise to God for His boundless grace, forgiveness, and love. We also need to be part of a group of men/women/couples, so we can gain support and serve when needed.

We should also financially support the ministries that the church supports, so yes, your wallet needs to *show up* as well. These are standard "member" issues where all should participate.

Let's take our showing up a notch. You can teach Sunday school and participate in worship as a musician, singer, or sound/video tech. Lead a small group of same aged folks or young adults, newly married, and the like. Also, help in the nursery. Direct traffic in the parking lot. Gardening, removing snow, patching holes in the parking lot are all great show-up moments. All these are very visible actions, and yes, there is sacrificial responsibility in those volunteer positions.

But let's look at the less-glamourous positions that every church needs someone to just show up. Clean up the sanctuary following worship. Pick up the trash, coffee cups, pens, and pencils, and leftover bulletins. Maybe pull out the carpet cleaner and suck up the coffee spilled around the facilities. Most of the time, no one is watching. Just show up and spend some time taking care of God's house.

Other areas of need include vacuuming during the week, washing windows, scrubbing the bathrooms, wiping down the nursery furniture and changing tables, and dusting the offices and classrooms.

I pastored a traveling church for many years. We met at a high school. There was someone to drive the trailer. Many helped in setting up the sound equipment, setting out Bibles, prepping the coffee. There were those who set up the classrooms and also put the furniture back in place.

I had a delightful lady show up every Thursday to print the bulletin, inserts, and the monthly newsletter. Sure, I could have done it, but it allowed me to do other things when she *showed up*.

I remember the dads who emailed me about worship setup. One was the father of two small girls. He wanted them to understand the issue of servanthood. So every week, the three showed up and set out the Bibles, offering baskets and information table.

Volunteering or showing up to help with Sunday school or youth programs can be frightening for some. Most of the time, the youth ministry model is loud, big personalities, high-energy games. This is me. I did this for years. Only recently, I had a thought, did this format attract *all the students* of the churches I served? Without question, the answer is *no*! The ones attracted were just like me: big personalities who loved adventure. There are others—quiet, low-energy board gamers who love high tech and sci-fi books and films—who don't usually make the mainstream. God made many flavors. We need to address each one.

My son-in-law, Whitney's widower, started working with the youth of his church. He is an engineer type who analyzes everything and loves the same things the aforementioned kids do. He is perfect for those kids. He can sit and chat about the latest sci-fi movie or event and discuss board-game strategies. He just started *showing up*, and now, there are kids who once sat on the margin who now see themselves as loved children of God.

Other than Sunday-morning needs, there are times when we can show up and help with the special holiday season programs and worship services. There are also summer and winter youth camps and vacation Bible school. Offer to work the kitchen, drive students, or set up lesson materials.

I know a former church family who spent many years in the gardening/nursery world. They had the talent and resources to decorate the sanctuary during Christmas and Easter. It was always beautiful and a tremendous example of showing up.

Here's something else to consider: most of the time, the pastors are men, and most of them are married. The pastor receives lots of attention, good and bad. What about their wives? Take her to breakfast or lunch. Become a friend.

Show up. The church needs you!

Chapter 13

A Friend Is Struggling—Show Up

This could cover many issues: breakup with a boy/girlfriend, divorce, loss of a pet, spiritual distress, or legal issues. This can be for a friend, or it can be with someone we don't know.

When flying around the United States alone, I am more perceptive to the needs of others around me. When I am with my family, I tend to their needs.

When traveling alone, I have been in airports and observed people crying or feeling seemingly depressed. They just had a hard phone call or serious text. Showing up can be as simple as asking someone, "Are you okay?" Some will pass it off as they are embarrassed or don't want a stranger to know their "stuff."

But there have been times when the individual has opened up and shared about the loss of a relationship or death. My job *done*.

I showed up and asked and then listened. For a few brief moments, they had a taste of kindness and compassion toward their struggle of grief. I usually try to end with a joke to put a smile on their face. Also, don't overstep your time.

Alyssa is a young lady I have known for nearly two decades. She recently shared this in her monthly missionary blog. I called her to discuss this story to be sure I had it right.

Alyssa shared:

> *After leaving a missionary assignment I journeyed to Switzerland to visit one of my friends. When I left her I set out for home, but I had a 17 hour layover in Paris. So I ventured out in the early morning to catch the sunrise at the Eiffel Tower and a few other places. During my excursion I met a girl named Maria.*
>
> *She and I hit it off at a coffee shop . . . talking about our favorite writers, showing each other photos from our time in the city and then we decided to go to the bookstore next door and see what we could find. We then meandered down the streets for a while before heading back to the airport to catch our flights. As we were going God have me a word of encouragement to share with her.*
>
> *She was stunned silent, because she didn't understand how I knew she needed to hear that. We then began talking more about Jesus and the gift of the Holy Spirit and what it means to be able to hear God's voice. She concluded with "While I know that there is a lot more for her it was a gift to be able to join Maria for a few hours in Paris."*

Alyssa just showed up and was obedient to the Holy Spirit to reach out and talk to Maria.[8]

My daughter Haley has a friend named Myranda. She once posted on social media about a couple of encounters she had at church with people she did not know. One involved a woman who began crying during the playing of a song. Myranda reached out and grabbed her shoulder. The lady told her that her brother had recently committed suicide and was very appreciative of her reaching out. Myranda showed up.

Myranda stated that it was a great reminder to be kind to one another as some strangers go through things that we can never imagine. They both wept together.

The second involved a woman texting on her phone during the entire worship service. Myranda thought, *She is missing a great message. Why be in church if you are just going to be texting the whole time?* Following the service, the woman apologized for being on her phone. She announced that during worship, she received an email that her biological mother and sister had been found. She had not seen them in over thirty years.

Myranda did nothing but show up and sit next to her. Then she became the first person to hear this news. They praised Jesus together and celebrated this great news. Sometimes showing up is all you have

---

[8] While this story originally appeared in written form, I spoke with Alyssa to confirm the details of the story and received permission to include in this book.

to do. The Holy Spirit will guide the encounter. Myranda showed up![9]

My wife, Carey, does this often. She reaches out and shows up in the life of other women—those going through divorce issues or dealing with special-needs children or substance abuse. The only cost to Carey was her time, but she has helped a wounded child of God find their path back to wholeness.

---

[9] These two stories originally appeared on social media. I reached out to Myranda to confirm the details and seek permission to include them in this book. By the way, I was honored, many months later, to officiate Myranda's wedding with John.

Chapter 14

Helping Those at Work—Show Up

This chapter is for the boss and the co-worker. Celebrate birthdays and anniversaries and support deaths in the lives of your co-workers and staff.

Many times, I have had staff who have had emergencies pop up: sick childcare provider, sick child or spouse or even parent, or flooding/fire at home. If you have a policy of allowing personal time off, use it. It may be titled as "vacation," so give them a few hours of vacation to attend to a broken-down car or court hearing.

During the first few months of grieving the loss of our daughter, the Collegiate Crossings board, staff, and a few local high school counselors stepped in and worked with our students. They kept the application and essay process moving forward until Carey and I could return to a normal workload.

If you don't have a policy, have the employee "punch out" and allow them to tend to the crisis off the clock. They may not get paid, but they know that they have a boss and co-workers who have their back when a predicament arises.

I had an amazing staff member who lost his wife. He had some vacation stocked up. Then it ran out. I told him to take the time off and let me know when he was ready to come back. He was gone for eight weeks. The entire staff discussed how to spread out his tasks, and all welcomed the opportunity to help.

The staff soon learned that we all were working with a "got your back" heart. Today, it is Bob or Sue. Tomorrow it may be me. There was no squabbling over work to do. In fact, we shut down the office, and all attended the funeral, driving through a wicked snowstorm. The whole staff *showed up*.

When I shared this with the HR company who worked with our company, they went nuts! "You can't do that!" Really? I just did! We went back and forth on how this should have been handled. I knew the guy was not going to budge, so I finally told him, "We are in the people business, helping them figure out their life and offering options to help them do so." I went on to say, "If we can't do that with our volunteers and paid staff, then we need to shut down and go do something else." Never heard a complaint again.

When my wife's parents passed several years ago, staff members from both of our places of work showed up and offered comfort. It was my first time to witness some of them in a dress or a coat and tie. Showing up was *huge*!

How else can this be played out at work?

- Bring your staff chips and salsa from a local restaurant just because. You can do this with popsicles and ice cream pops as well.
- In the summer, announce free lunch Saturdays or BBQ or sub sandwiches for staff and volunteers.

Sure, these things cost. Plan your budget accordingly and realize that the $20 to $50 spent on your staff is chicken feed compared to the goodwill created.

Other ways to show up and let your staff know you care and you are looking out for them include the following:

- Call an employee into your office just to tell them "good job." Better yet, announce the good job in front of other staff. This can be huge for the individual and also serve as motivation for others to do well.
- When you know a staff member is hurting physically or emotionally, come alongside and give a hug or a pat on the back, assuring them you are on the journey with them. Take them for coffee or send them home early to compose themselves. Hugs may not be Politically Correct. Remember, Jesus was not PC!
- Provide a gift card at the holidays. This is a great gesture, and it doesn't go against their payroll and cost them on their tax return.
- Go out to the parking lot and wash the windows of your staff's cars.
- Once a year, take your staff to lunch individually to see how they are doing in the job, family, and personal life.

This is more casual—a nice blessing of a good meal and an opportunity for your staff to see you in a different light.
- Show up when a baby is born. This has been discussed earlier. Bring dinner to the family. Take the burden of cooking off their
- Assuming children are allowed in the office or work place, let the kids and families stop by on occasion to say hi to Mom or Dad. This takes away the mystery of what parents do for a living.
- Allow children to sell scout cookies or school candy at work as long as it doesn't conflict with work. You may need to schedule this properly as several kids might do this kind of fundraising.
- I could fill pages with ideas. Create something that fits your staff!

Most of this costs you zero dollars. By you being open and allowing your staff to participate with their family and other issues of interest, you are supporting them in a way they have never been supported. You showed up and offered your staff new ways to understand they are loved and cared for.

Chapter 15

Helping Organizations—Show Up

There are nonprofits, churches, youth programs, sports programs, environmental groups, and animal associations that always need help.

Collectively, for thirteen years, my wife and I both worked for Habitat for Humanity. She raised funds. I ran a ReStore. A ReStore is a thrift shop that generates funds to help families in need to build houses they turn into homes. The ReStore and many charitable retail thrift shops need volunteers for unloading and loading, mopping, merchandising, and cleaning bathrooms. Yes, they have staff, but the work can be daunting.

When I took over as manager of the ReStore, there was a signup list for volunteers. I did away with the signup list. Why? If they had completed our orientation, then they were invited to come when they were available. There were times when volunteers, all of a sudden, had a few hours to serve. This benefited the charity and the volunteer as many were putting in hours for restitution, assigned by a judge, or working required hours to receive government subsidies, such as food, utility bill payment, or rent. This is a double *show up*.

The ReStore needed the help, and the volunteer needed the hours. Some of those volunteers eventually worked their way into a paid job. By doing away with the signup sheets, we took a roadblock out of volunteering. Are there any obstacles to overcome to help someone or a group? Is there a barrier that keeps others away from helping you? Find a way to make it happen and bless someone.

The humane society needs dog walkers and kennel cleaners. Hospitals need greeters and those to help visitors find the correct floor and rooms for procedures or finding patients.

Youth sport programs need coaches, scoreboard operators, and scorebook keepers.

Did you play sports in the past? Contact the YMCA, town recreation programs, Little League, or youth football. Most don't have the resources to pay coaches. Use your experience and knowledge of the sport to help the next generation. This is another example of sacrificial responsibility. Fill a need!

What about hospice? The scouts? Meals on Wheels? Community home repair groups?

I have never heard of or worked at a charitable organization that wasn't desperately in need of volunteers. There is so much good that needs to be accomplished in our world, but the resources (financial and human) are almost always lacking.

For most nonprofit organizations, this could be their motto: "If you're available, we have a need. No experience required."

Show up. They need you!

Chapter 16

Local School—Show Up

This chapter is for administrators, teachers, and students, many of whom show up every day to care and teach the next generation of community leaders. This is also for those who are "retired" or have a flexible schedule, allowing them opportunities to reach out and serve.

Millions of people are in school every day: elementary, secondary, and college or university. Many times, teachers see and interact with younger children more than their parents do.

Many schools have kindhearted folks who look after marginalized kids. They check in on the "wallflowers" and make sure kids look like they have eaten and have a healthy physical presence, with no excessive bruises, broken bones, or cuts and scrapes.

Sadly, it is possible that some are being abused. There are others who are very physical and play sports or play hard on the playground, and their bodies have a lot of wear and tear.

Our middle daughter was a competitive cheerleader. She had joint dislocations, concussions, broken bones, and bruises. We are still wondering why someone didn't call Child Protect Services to have her checked out. Haley was just a very physical child participating in lots of athletics and general play. Most staff and school faculty understood this about Haley, but they still checked to be sure she was okay.

Be on the lookout for kids who eat lunch by themselves and those who don't seem to have enough to eat. Most school districts and schools in the United States have a free/reduced-lunch program. Many also do breakfast. If there is a need, direct the family to these resources.

Be on the lookout for behavioral changes in students, young and old. Did something happen at home: divorce, abuse, arrest, or drug use?

Some kids miss a lot of school for many reasons. They sleep too late or are regularly sick. Maybe they were needed that day to help with the family business. If someone misses a couple of days in a row, give a call or send a text or email. You may also stop by with homework from that day while checking up on their well-being.

Make it a point to seek out the "new kid." There are lots of worries and concerns a newbie experiences. There could be language issues, cultural issues, and general knowledge about the school and community you can help them with.

Teachers and administrators, you could develop a group of students to be the welcome wagon of your classroom or school. When a new student arrives, direct your student group to that student with the intent of service, such as pointing out the bathroom, cafeteria, school policies, clubs, and sports.

I know several students who pack their lunch and a snack or two. For some, snack time is *huge*: cookies, pretzels, string cheeses, fruit, and chips. It is something to help tide someone over until lunch or the end of the day. If there is a set snack time at school and someone is without, it may because of a financial issue. If you have the resources, pack some more to share. My daughters did this for years. Cheddar Goldfish was always a hit!

I know teachers who keep packaged snacks on hand for those kids in need.

My mom was the K-8 school lunch lady when I was younger. It had its benefits as I grew older. She realized that so much food was being thrown away. If there was something served that day that could be wrapped and saved, she did it.

I was surprised as a kid that the school charged the same amount for an early-elementary school lunch as they did for a middle schooler. A six-year-old and a twelve-year-old have far different needs. So when she could "save" a sandwich, slice of pizza, apple, or orange, she would. Sometimes the pile was large. She would then give this food to the bigger kids who needed it or the ones who may only eat lunch that day.

Elementary schools can use volunteers to help kids with their reading, arithmetic, and penmanship. Purchase decks of flash cards and work with the children who struggle with math or reading. Very little cost, just time. This is great for those who are retired and are looking for something to do each day. It gives one purpose—a reason to get out of bed each morning.

Some teachers keep a spotless classroom. It is their pride and joy. Then there are others... not so much pride. Offer to come in and scrub and clean once a month. Sure, there are janitors who dump trash, sweep, and run a quick rag over the classroom; but they don't have the time to do a deep clean until the summer break. Show up with a rag, squirt bottle, and a little elbow grease. You will be applauded for your efforts!

One issue that never gets old anywhere, especially at a school, is thank-you notes. Send a positive email or handwritten note to teachers, janitors, staff, and administrators. While your children or grandchildren may not attend the local school, you can still show up for those in the local school as they are educating the future of our country.

At school, there are so many ways to come alongside others. Show up. Everyone needs a friend or an apple.

Chapter 17

Prison Visits—Show Up

In the Mathew 25 (sheep and goats), Jesus confirms the actions of those who feed the hungry, clothe the naked, house the homeless, offer a drink to the thirsty, and care for those who are sick. There is one more issue discussed: visit those in prison.

Whoa, whoa, whoa, the Lord wants us to go to prison and sit with those convicted of a crime? Yes!

Too often, we find ourselves offended by the actions of others. Instead of proclaiming their crime or misdeed as a reason to shun them and responding with harsh words, we are called to apply the principle of giving a kind word or response to those who have been incarcerated for their actions: *"A gentle answer turns away wrath, but a harsh word stirs up anger"* (Prov. 15:1).

We are also called to extend tender mercies: *"Therefore, as God's chosen people, holy and dearly loved, clothe yourselves with compassion, kindness, humility, gentleness and patience"* (Col. 3:12).

The Evil One would like us to hang on to angry thoughts about others, hold a grudge against a brother, or keep a resentful attitude toward anyone who has wronged us or someone we love.

Jesus wants us to remember Matthew 18:35: "*This is how my heavenly Father will treat each of you [handing you over to jailers and tortured, or wrongdoing] unless you forgive your brother or sister from your heart.*" Just as the Lord forgives each of us from the heart, He wants us to learn to forgive others in the same generous, merciful way.

As a father, husband, pastor, and church leader, I have messed up! Sometimes my words are un-Christ-like and hurtful. Sadly, I can be funny at the expense of someone else.

I am glad for forgiveness of those under my care and the church as a whole. This holds true for when I have wronged my family or friends. We are called to offer the same forgiveness and care to those who have committed crimes, though they may still be paying their debt to society while incarcerated for years to come.

The Lord tells us plainly in Micah 6:8, "*He has shown you, O mortal, what is good. And what does the L<small>ORD</small> require of you? To act justly and to love mercy and to walk humbly with your God.*"

So What Does This Look Like?

Due to security issues, most people can't just show up at a prison and ask for entry. My personal experience is to work with a noted prison ministry.

- Prison Fellowship
- Angel Tree

- God Behind Bars

While I have a general understanding of how all these work, my direct involvement has been with God Behind Bars.

Through our local congregation, the Department of Corrections, and God Behind Bars, every week, we bring worship and fellowship to a level 4 prison in Colorado. There is plenty of training to understand the dos and don'ts and expectations of this work.

Volunteers show up every week to spend time with the inmates. Not all inmates are allowed to attend, which is sad but understandable. It is pretty simple: show up and be a friend and prayer partner.

I have never asked an inmate *why* they are there or *how long* they will be locked up. To me, it doesn't matter. We are called to love them and offer Jesus.

Sure, some have offered this info, but it is not necessary to ask as we are there to offer love and care for men who are hurting physically, emotionally, and spiritually. This work is not about judging one's actions.

At Christmas, a family event brings the inmates and their families together for a night of gifts, food, and worship. Recently, only twenty-eight men were allowed to participate out of a prison population of nearly one thousand. Those rules and guidelines for participation are set by the Department of Corrections. Of those twenty-eight, only three have hope of ever leaving the prison.

So why do this? Why bother? As they may be physically shackled for the crimes they committed, the ministry offers spiritual freedom through Christ Jesus.

Too often, we in the church think we need to *fix* someone of their wrongs. We have to stop and realize that we are equally sinful, hurtful, and wrong. We just may not have been caught by law enforcement.

In the eyes of the Lord, sin is sin. We have *all* fallen short of God's perfect plan. The Lord knows our actions, thoughts, and ways.

We are called to show up and offer love and mercy even to those wearing a solid colored jumpsuit with a number stenciled on the chest pocket.

The *most* amazing part of this work is it is not just the prisoners who are blessed by this relationship.

I had a fellow volunteer offer this story:

> A dear lady and her husband had been volunteering for a few months, and her normal practice was to inquire from the inmates how she could pray for them.
>
> One week, an inmate shared his prayer request. He then asked her what he and his fellow prayer warriors could lift up in prayer for her. She was nervous to answer as much of the training the volunteers go through emphasizes the need for anonymity. After a few moments, she gave in and said, "Please pray for our prodigal son. He has been away from the Lord for a long time." They parted ways as it was time for

worship. Upon the conclusion, the inmate came to her and stated that he and others had lifted her son up in prayer. She was pleased and felt blessed.

The next afternoon the woman's son called her. He lives out of state, and they had not been in contact for many months. He announced that he woke that morning and felt compelled to take the family to church! When the altar call came, he stepped forward and accepted Christ!

In the next couple of weeks, the son's wife accepted Jesus, and both were baptized! And now they are looking for ways to share Jesus with co-workers and friends.

The mom had to wait for a few weeks to share this with the prisoners who had prayed for her son as there is a volunteer rotation. When she did, several "hardened" prisoners were in tears as they had added to the kingdom!

Even in the shackles of prison, they can find freedom in Christ Jesus.

Visiting those in prison is a hard task. There are forms to fill out, background checks, travel to the prison, and the worry and anxiety of being "locked up." This is not for the faint of heart, but we are still called to *show up*.

I know some business people who seek to hire those who have been incarcerated. Their heart is calling them to give someone a second chance. They defeat the argument that you are to keep work at work and faith at church. But then, we are reminded that faith is our life—our whole life. To this argument, they offer, "I don't care about your past. Let's look to the future. If Jesus can forgive me, you too can be forgiven."

We are called to feed the hungry, clothe the naked, shelter the homeless, give a drink to the thirsty, tend to the sick, and visit the imprisoned. We can be a blessing to them, and those incarcerated can be a blessing to everyone else inside and outside the prison.

Chapter 18

Your Family—Show Up

This may seem to obvious but not for many.

This area of concern could be a book itself! I saved this show-up topic for last on purpose.

God has entrusted a small group of people to our care: our family. This is for both dads and moms, as well as siblings, aunts, and uncles. For pastors, family is our first congregation!

Parents are gifted with different talents, passions, and abilities; but they are to be used for the same purpose: serve, love, and care for those we have been charged to bless, who are our children and each other.

Biblically, moms and dads are called to turn their hearts to the Lord before they can expect their children to have faith in God. Parents need to lead the way. We need to be followers of the Lord before we can expect our children to do so.

When we turn our hearts to God, we become more aware of those around us and the needs of our family. We know their needs and act upon them. Then they will turn their hearts to us just as God had intended.

While this challenge is for both mom and dad to show up and share their faith, the scripture is specific to the role of dads! The father is to be the leader!

"Husbands, love your wives, just as Christ loved the church and gave himself up for her" (Eph. 5:25). Sacrifice.

"Fathers, do not exasperate your children; instead, bring them up in the training and instruction of the Lord" (Eph. 6:4). Discipleship.

You've probably heard people say, "My wife and I have agreed that we don't want to force our religion/faith upon our children. We don't want to put pressure on them to quickly make up their minds on matters as important as religion."

This may sound wise or loving, but *no*, it is abdicating one's calling as a parent. If you are a Christian, you need to share Jesus! You can't have a religious neutrality in the home because taking a neutral stance about God is itself a form of religion. This can lead to agnostic or atheistic attitudes toward God. If there is a detachment attitude from parents to children toward God, then that is the most likely position of their children. Most parents see the validity in sharing their thoughts about money, health, education, or who they root for in the NFL; but to be overly *open minded* about God is in direct opposition to Paul's writing to the Ephesians (above).

Children may follow what we say but are more likely to follow what we do. Fathers are called to be men of faith so that their children have someone on this earth to follow.

When your kids are little, tuck them in at night and attend all their school functions, even parent-teacher conferences. Not enough dads attend these. They don't know what is going on with their child's education. Get to know their teachers and administrators.

Find out what interests them and then participate: sports, scouts, dance, music, art, and science. Dads, have a tea party with your daughter, and *yes*, allow her to do your hair and makeup!

Many years ago, when our girls were young, they would frequently paint my toenails. Messy but colorful! One morning, following an evening "salon" session, I was participating in a staff meeting at the church. I was warm, and I slipped off my shoes. I was wearing sockless slip-on loafers. My toes were exposed. The senior pastor sat directly across from me. His face soon displayed an unusual expression. He saw the nail polish! I quickly slipped my shoes back on and stated, "I'm a good dad." He laughed. He and his wife raised three boys, no girls. Sometimes you do for others something unusual, but that means you showed up.

Listen to your kid's stories. You will learn about their joy, pain, worries, and fears. You will hear names of friends, allowing you to contact the parents to simply say hello.

Doing this, you just showed up in another child's life, and now you have someone else to bless, and that family can come to you with blessing as well.

When it comes time to actually pray, I would suggest you open the prayer but invite your children to participate as well. They learn to pray what is on their heart for family, friends, and the world when you teach them and then give them the opportunity to bring it to Jesus!

As your children age, there will be more school projects, sports, dances. This is when the serious talks need to begin, such as dating relationships or proper manners in treating a girl/boy. These two are often missed.

They are missed as they make some people uncomfortable. Remember, you were called to parent, not remain comfortable in the big issues of life. You are to be a parent. Sure, you can be friendly, but be a parent, not your child's best friend, when they are young.

Take them on errands and discuss life as it unfolds around you. On that short trip to the store, car repair shop, or dry cleaners, point things out and talk. Talk about chemical dependency issues or finances. Teach them to drive! Review the latest world, national, and state issues and how they affect them and their friends.

Here's a *huge* issue: teach them how to cook! You *show up* and show them how to make cookies, mac and cheese, grill, pancakes, and eggs. Not only will they now *not* starve, but they will also be a blessing to a future spouse.

I know. You don't have the time because of work. *Yes*, you have to work to keep the bills paid and provide what your children need. Keep the amount of work hours to a reasonable length. Sure, your job could use you for fifty to sixty hours a week. Are you being paid for that many hours? My guess is *no*. If you cut back the hours to something more manageable, the other hours now become your hours for your family.

This goes both ways, Mom and Dad. If this puts your job in jeopardy, keep in mind, who do you want raising your children? Carey and I have had to make that decision. It's a tough one.

Not long ago, NFL and MLB teams came calling. I was asked if I was interested in becoming their next PA announcer. Wow, what an honor. The problem is, Carey and I would have to move out of state and leave our kids and extended family. We took a pass. Since then, several other opportunities have arisen, some requiring only local travel or occasional road trips.

I have heard the argument that the extra hours are needed for retirement, new home addition, or a nice trip. All those are great and understandable. But are they necessary?

Most Families Need Less Money and More Mom and Dad!

A friend of mine and I recently chatted about this. He stated that for twenty years, he had been chasing the big dollars offered by corporate America. He went on say that he has learned that he needs to "give more of me to my kids and wife, the school, and community." He has discovered the value of *showing up* in the lives of those God has entrusted to him.

Go to their school or offer to help at dances, games, concerts, overnights, and the like. Show up!

When it is time to plan for their postsecondary education (college), show up.

Lots of decisions, lots of money. Participate. Guide them through the process. If you have no clue what to do, there are some great resources that your child's school can provide. But be involved. Show up.

Help them move into their new college dorm or apartment.

Help them move home over the summer, or to another location if they are taking a job near the school or take an internship out of state.

My wife and I have had longtime relationships with our girl's friends. Now that they are adults, we have had the opportunity to be involved in wedding showers and ceremonies, baby showers, and blessings. Showing up in the lives of your children's friends blesses you and builds up another family who needed to see Jesus.

When your children marry and have children, be at the hospital for the delivery! Be first in line to watch the grandchildren on anniversaries, three-day weekends, or when Mom or Dad is sick or needs to be out of town for work. Attend the events of the grandkids. They can fill your social calendar quickly!

A small group friend recently shared with me an idea he had for his grandson. The young man was soon to be turning thirteen years old and he wanted to offer 'a rite of passage' camping trip with his father, uncles and a couple of other family members. This would include some survival adventures, fishing and sleeping outdoors. There would also be some Bible lessons along the journey. He hadn't worked out all the details, he just wanted affirmation that this was good idea. No, not a good idea… a GREAT one! If you have grandchildren consider this…if you don't… plan on something like this. The children of today are the leaders of tomorrow… speak into their lives the lessons of scripture. Speak into their lives how much they are loved and how they are a precious gift from God. I do this every time I am with Hudson. When I conclude this little affirmation, I conclude with 'Papa loves you.' He responds in a soft voice… 'I love you too Papa.' My heart melts-every time.

We recently moved from one part of town to another—same zip code. In our new neighborhood, several older couples uprooted themselves from all over the country and moved into our neighborhood. The number one reason: to be closer to the grandkids. Well done!

If your children or grandchildren live out of state, you can still have contact. Text them or make a Facebook post for birthdays, extracurricular activities, grades, or other special accomplishments at school or work. With the advent of social media platforms, Zoom, Skype, and the like, staying in contact is easy.

Carey and I have one grandchild. Before he was born, we had already started stocking up on kids' stuff and making plans for when they come to the house, such as blocks, toys, cars, and trucks and musical instruments. This also meant refurbishing the cradle I crafted over thirty years ago. For the first few months, Hudson slept in the same bed that his mom and aunts had slept. My daughters are scared.

If you don't show up for your family, who will?

Chapter 19

Let's Dock This Boat

In Genesis 3:16–19, God curses the woman's body because of her sin, but he curses the creation that man was meant to cultivate because of his sin. This is why small groups in a church or any ministry setting are so needed as they are used to encourage and come alongside and love one another because life is hard! Life is full of death, loss, and grief.

But have you ever wondered, "Wouldn't it be better if, when we got saved, God took all the adversities and trials away and gave us an easy life so that others would want to follow Jesus as well and be saved?" Nope, there are several reasons. Here are a few:

- That's idol worship. If I come to Jesus just to get an easy life, then the easy life is my god, and I'm just using Jesus to get it. That's the prosperity gospel. "Just go to church, carry a *big* Bible, and trust God will give your desires. You will have earthly riches, money, cars, homes, jets, jewels."

- We tend to ignore God when all is well and only press into Him when things aren't going so well for us. It seems we are open to the Holy Spirit when times are tough, but when there is an abundance, we like to take credit and think that others need to get their act together.

Statistically, when the United States is at war or there has been a major crisis, such as WWII, Middle East conflicts, and 9/11, church attendance jumps, and church financial giving goes up as well. Sadly, within a couple of months, the numbers start to slide; and within six months, the numbers are back to where they were before the issue that drove us to Jesus.

Life is hard. It's best to do it with others who have the same heart, who are servants or image bearers who understand sacrificial responsibility.

We began by looking at Paul's letter to the church of Philippi in chapter 2. Let's finish there:

> *Therefore, my dear friends, as you have always obeyed—not only in my presence, but now much more in my absence—continue to work out your salvation with fear and trembling, for it is God who works in you to will and to act in order to **fulfill his good purpose** (Phil. 2:12–13).*

We were created to be *one* with God. We have been created to fulfill His *good purpose*. We were created to serve others. All these are because we are the image bearers of God.

If the church, its people, doesn't take on the sacrificial responsibility for God's creation, who will?

Show up. Everyone needs you!

One Last Word

Whitney attained her MA in elementary education online through Grand Canyon University. She completed her student teaching at a culturally and economically diverse elementary school in the greater Seattle area back in early 2015.

She learned to deal with various personalities, cultures, and socioeconomic students. Whitney was very loved as she showed up for her students every day.

Toward the end of her time at the school, a new student was welcomed into the classroom. This young man said very little, seem depressed most days, and related to very few other students.

She soon discovered that his family had recently migrated to the United States from Eastern Europe, and now they were settling in the Seattle area. There were language and culture issues. He was one of at least six kids, and the family had very few resources.

After discovering that this young man rarely had anything to eat for breakfast, Whitney worked to place him and his siblings on the free reduced-lunch program. That seemed to help as he was a bit more energetic following lunch. But the same demeanor showed up each morning. It seems there was very little food at home for breakfast or dinner.

The school had a weekend take-home backpack food plan. Someone would donate nonperishable food to the school district, and it would be sent home on Fridays to help the families in need.

The backpack was stuffed with dry cereal, canned goods, dry milk, and the like. While this helped, it still was not enough as there were nearly ten mouths to feed in this young man's household.

The second week, Whitney supplemented the take-home food with more cereal and canned goods. This was still not enough.

Whitney called us to see if Carey and I could help. Sure! We wrote Whit a few checks to go out and buy more cereal, veggies, bread, and meat!

Most of this extra food would not fit in the backpack, so she helped him to the bus with the bags.

On the coming Monday, the young man bolted into the classroom with a million-dollar smile. He ran to Whitney and hugged her with all his might.

He then backed up and shouted in his broken English, "We got to eat! We had food!" This was followed by more hugs and tears.

Those tears show up every time I retell this story.

Whitney showed up.

Resources

Max Lucado It's Not About Me: Rescue From the Life We Thought Would Make Us Happy THOMAS NELSON / 2011 / HARDCOVER

Robert Greenleaf Greenleaf Center 133 Peachtree Street, NE - Lobby Suite 350

Atlanta, GA 30303

Robert Lupton
Toxic Charity How the Church Hurts Those They Help and How to Reverse it
New York: HarperCollins Publishers/2011

Author, lecturer Doug Wilson
FamilyLife
P.O. Box 7111
Little Rock, AR 72223
www.FamilyLife.com

Rachel's Challenge
7901 Southpark Plaza #210

Littleton, CO 80120
303.470.3000

God Behind Bars 241 North Stephanie St Henderson, NV 89074 Info@GodBehindBars.com

Whitney's Blog Our family started a blog in Whitney's name a few months after her passing. Most of it are reflections and life lessons from her life. The first year, it contained a weekly posting. It is now monthly. It can also be found on the immediate family's personal Facebook pages. Check it out and be encouraged: whitneyswalk.weebly.com

New International Version – Bible 3900 Sparks Dr. SE Grand Rapids, MI 49546 (all scripture quoted within this text is from the NIV, unless otherwise noted.)

About the Author

Andy McClure is the father to three daughters, two on earth and one in heaven. He and his wife, Carey, have been married for over thirty years. Andy is a graduate of Fuller Theological Seminary and Northern Arizona University. He spent over ten years in broadcasting, predominantly in news/talk radio. After feeling called to full-time ministry, he served three churches over an eighteen-year period. Currently, Andy and Carey run a nonprofit college access organization (Collegiate Crossings), working with all students to help them navigate the postsecondary education admission process. The heart of the mission is to help low-income and first-generation students create a future that will support their family and community. The intent is to break the cycle of poverty through education. Andy also serves the Olympics, NCAA, and high school and club sports as a public address announcer throughout Colorado, around the United States, and world.

Afterword

In the first few minutes immediately following Whitney's passing, many showed up at the hospital. Both sides of Carey's and Andy's immediate family started showing up. Then they started showing up at the house. Most were local, but many from out of state started arriving within twelve hours. What a blessing! There are so many who showed up. Thank you!

Beards
Beavers
Bertarellis
Bixbys
Chandlers
Estlers
Feddemas
Gannett-Matthews
Geubelles
Geyers
Reesers
Schoenwieses
Wilsons

CPSIA information can be obtained
at www.ICGtesting.com
Printed in the USA
JSHW022013240622
27316JS00003B/12